Published by Sweet Cherry Publishing Limited
Unit 36, Vulcan House,
Vulcan Road,
Leicester, LE5 3EF
United Kingdom

First published in the US in 2022
2022 edition

2 4 6 8 10 9 7 5 3 1

ISBN: 978-1-80263-047-3

© Harry Meredith

Soccer Rising Stars: Kai Havertz

Cover design and illustrations
by Sophie Jones

Lexile® code numerical measure L = Lexile® 950L

www.sweetcherrypublishing.com

Printed and bound in Turkey

KAI HAVERTZ

THE UNOFFICIAL STORY

Written by
HARRY MEREDITH

Sweet Cherry

CONTENTS

1. First to Thirty Goals!   7

2. Grandad's Influence   15

3. Alemannia Aachen   21

4. The Boy at Bayer   29

5. Exams vs Champions League   37

6. Die Mannschaft   47

7. Top Scoring Midfielder   56

8. Jack of All Trades   64

9. London Bound   78

10. Positive   89

11. Perfection in Porto   99

12. Euro 2020   108

13. Road to Qatar 2022   123

1

FIRST TO THIRTY GOALS!

Fans waved their red-and-black flags as players emerged from the BayArena tunnel and onto the field. Bayer 04 Leverkusen were playing a league match at home against

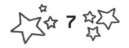

Eintracht Frankfurt. Bayer had a small chance of making it into the top four of the 2019/2020 Bundesliga table: a position that would make sure they qualified for the Champions League.

At first glance, this match was not one for fans to get too excited about. But with the help of Bayer's young star Kai Havertz, it would be written down in the Bundesliga history books.

Bayer's number 29 led the team onto the field. Kai looked around the stadium at the thousands of fans there to cheer on his team. He was going to make sure that they did not leave the

BayArena disappointed. It was time for Kai Havertz to put on a show.

In the 4th minute of the match, Bayer's Moussa Diaby sprinted down the left. His red-hot speed was too much for the defenders and he whizzed past them with ease. He fired a cross into the box, where Kai had made a run. The ball moved at such a speed that it seemed it would pass Kai completely. Before Kai knew it, the ball was flying across

 him and he couldn't reach it with his favored left foot. Instead, Kai quickly

 stuck out his right leg and connected with the ball. *Goal!* It struck the back of the net and Kai joined his teammates in celebration.

Not only had Kai scored the opening goal for his team, but he'd just broken a Bundesliga record. He was now the youngest ever player to reach thirty Bundesliga goals at 20 years and 270 days old.

It wasn't long before Bayer added to their lead. In the 14th minute Paulinho, making his first Bundesliga start for the team, made a smart run into the box. The midfielder passed the ball across the goal and Karim Bellarabi tapped in the team's second goal. The score stayed the same for the rest of the first half. After extra time had been played, the referee blew his whistle and the teams headed to the changing rooms.

Kai's teammates came over to him in the changing room, patting him on the back and congratulating him. Before their manager Peter Bosz gave his thoughts on the game, he wanted to applaud Kai.

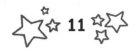

"Well played, boys," said Bosz. "But first I think we need to give a little shout out. Kai, up you get."

Kai, holding in his laughter, stood up bashfully.

"This kid has just broken a record. He deserves a round of applause."

The rest of the team got to their feet and clapped for him. Many of them cheered and whistled, with Bellarabi even squirting a water bottle at Kai as if it were champagne during a cup final celebration.

"Thanks, I think," Kai laughed, drying his wet hair with a towel.

Kai and Bayer carried their winning attitude into the second half of the match. In the 49th minute, they increased their lead to 3-0 with a cross-goal shot from the energetic Paulinho. Kai even played his part by scoring a fourth goal for Bayer.

In the 55th minute, Kai was on the edge of the opposition box and surrounded by defenders. He played a delicate through ball into the area. It left every defender helpless, with no other option but to watch as Paulinho scored another goal for Bayer, taking the score to 4-0. Bayer cruised to victory and ended what had appeared to be an ordinary match with three points, four goals and a new record. If Kai could achieve all of this at just 20 years old, what could he achieve throughout the rest of his career?

2
GRANDAD'S INFLUENCE

Kai Havertz arrived in the world on the 11th of June 1999. He was the third child after his sister Leah and brother Jan. His mother was a successful lawyer and his father a hard working police officer. Both of his parents liked soccer, with his father playing

as an amateur in his youth. But Kai got his passion for soccer from another member of the family.

At the age of 4, Kai was often running around in the back garden tightly holding his favorite stuffed donkey. Kai was obsessed with donkeys. He liked them so much that he wanted his own donkey farm when he grew up. That way, he could play with the animals whenever he wanted to. In the garden one day, he was playing pretend when a familiar voice called him from the kitchen.

"Kai!" said his grandad.

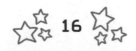

Kai rushed to the kitchen door,
and his grandad ruffled his hair. Kai's
grandad stepped down into the garden
and walked onto the grass. Tucked
underneath his arm was a soccer
ball. Kai's grandad loved soccer. He'd
played all his life, and while his body
had grown tired, his passion for soccer
had never faded. He was now the long-
serving chairman of a local soccer
team: Alemannia Mariadorf.

"Here you go," said Kai's grandad,
chucking the ball to Kai.
The 4-year-old quickly
reacted and controlled

the ball, bringing it down to the ground before passing it back. His granddad stood there, amazed.

"That was good!" he said. "I wouldn't believe you're only 4 if I didn't know any better. Would you like to play more soccer?"

Kai nodded.

"Well, you know, I spend my days running a soccer club. We actually have a special team for kids just like you. Now, I'll have to ask your parents first. But—"

Before Kai's grandad could ask, Kai had placed his stuffed donkey on the

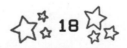

ground and was running around the garden with the ball.

"I'll take that as a yes then," said Kai's grandad, laughing.

Kai kicked the ball against the shed and slid on his knees.

"Goooaaalllll!"

Kai joined Alemannia Mariadorf. It was clear from the start that he had talent. During his time with the club, he often played with age groups two years above him. Even alongside older players, who were bigger and more experienced, Kai stood out. Kai continued to develop at Alemannia Mariadorf as a junior, and it was not long before higher tier teams came calling.

ALEMANNIA AACHEN

In 2009, at the age of 10, Kai was
invited to join Alemannia Aachen's
youth academy. At the time, the
club was an impressive side in the 2.
Bundesliga: Germany's second best
professional soccer league. They were
just one good season away from being

promoted to the same division as the likes of Bayern Munich and Borussia Dortmund.

While Kai enjoyed playing for his grandad's team, he knew joining Alemannia Aachen was an opportunity he couldn't turn down. His family thought the same and encouraged him to move. The step up to a professional team gave Kai the facilities, coaches and training he needed to develop at a rate that matched his potential. The club were the biggest in the region by far, and the move meant that Kai could continue to play at a higher level but stay close to home.

Kai settled into his new surroundings very quickly. He became a passionate fan of the professional team and often watched them play in their league matches. He cheered on the team's stars such as striker Erik Meijer, hoping to one day play alongside them.

At the academy, Kai continued where he left off with Alemannia Mariadorf. He quickly progressed through the ranks and carried on playing for teams in older age groups. One of these matches would have an incredible impact on the young player's career.

Kai had been chosen to play for Alemannia Aachen's under 12s. The team were coming up against a tough and well-run club: Bayer 04 Leverkusen. They were an established Bundesliga side who had an impressive crop of academy players. Kai would be going up against them.

The Alemannia Aachen coach brought his players into a huddle on the field. Kai, one of the smallest on the team, squeezed in between his teammates.

"I want you to go out there and give me your all today," said the coach. "They might be a big name, but you're big game players. Go and do us all proud." The coach moved into the middle of the circle.

"On three. One, two, three!" said the coach.

"Come on!" roared the players.

Kai and his teammates carried this passion into the game, but they were in for a tough match. Bayer

scored the first goal, the second, the
third, then a fourth and before long,
a fifth. Despite this score, Kai and
his teammates never gave up. Kai
grabbed a goal back for his team, and
soon after he scored a second. In a
ten-minute spell of the match, he was
easily the best player on the field.

Kai stole the ball and ran through
the Bayer midfield alone, keeping
the ball closely under his control.
He dribbled past defenders before
smashing the ball with his left foot
into the net and scoring a hat trick.
Although they were still losing,

Kai's teammates surrounded him
and celebrated.

"Kai, Kai, Kai!" They all chanted.

On the bench, the Bayer manager
looked at the Aachen coach with his
hands on his head in amazement. The
Aachen coach could only smile back
at him.

Despite Kai's heroic display,
Aachen went on to lose the match
8-3. Although they lost, the team had
done themselves proud by playing to
the best of their abilities. At times Kai
had been the best player on the field
and everyone knew it.

Before this game, top clubs had been monitoring Kai's progress. There were rumors swirling around about a once-in-a-generation talent who was emerging from the region. Although Bayer had won the match, there was only one thought on the Bayer coach's mind:

We must sign Kai Havertz.

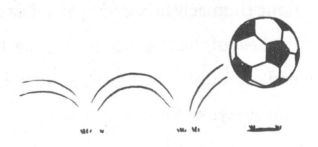

4

THE BOY AT BAYER

After only a year with Alemannia Aachen, Kai was on the move once again. At age 13, his talent had outgrown the club, and he needed to be tested against the best. Bayer 04 Leverkusen were a big-name side founded in 1904. At their academy,

Kai was going to be taught by some of the country's top soccer coaches.

Kai's first move to Alemannia Aachen was close to home. Fortunately, the Bayer training facility was still close enough to travel to, so Kai could live at home with his family. Hour-long journeys soon became a part of the Havertz family's weekly routine. Kai's parents, their friends and extended family all helped out so that Kai could get to training. But being on the road a lot wasn't a new experience for the family. Kai's home of Mariadorf was not many miles away from the Dutch border. In years past, he had often taken part in tournaments in the Netherlands. His parents did everything they could to make sure he could play against the best competition and develop his skills. Now it was finally paying off.

Kai slotted into life in Leverkusen well. Despite being one of the smallest players on the team, he continued to impress the coaches. He quickly progressed at the academy over a couple of years. But eventually, changes in his size began to hold him back. Over the space of his U16 year, Kai went from being one of the shortest players on the team to one of the tallest.

Kai's father dropped him off at the training facility one day. With his cleat bag in his hand, Kai crossed the concrete parking lot and made his way to the changing rooms. Kai pushed open the door. As he entered one of his teammates gawped at him, his eyes wide and his water bottle falling to the floor.

"You've shot up again!" said his teammate. "What are they feeding you?"

Kai laughed. "I don't know what's happening!"

"You'll be taller than the coaches soon," said Kai's teammate.

At the age of 15, Kai was no longer a small, technical attacker, but a rangy midfielder. While the growth spurt brought pros like improved strength and heading opportunities, it also came with cons. Kai had to get used to a body much different to how it used to be. It almost felt as though the feet and legs he was playing with were someone else's.

His proportions had changed so suddenly that for a while Kai struggled to regain his strong form. Alongside these troubles, changing at such a pace caused tremendous growing pains for Kai. He had to deal with that pain as well as getting used to his changing body. Eventually, Kai got to grips with the changes and returned to his impressive soccer form.

In 2016, Kai helped lead the U17 Bayer 04 Leverkusen team in a season to remember. He played an important part in helping them be

 crowned U17 German Bundesliga champions. Kai scored an amazing eighteen goals during the season and impressed everyone that watched him play. He performed so well that he was recognized by the German Football Association.

Every year, at the end of the season, the best young players in Germany are given either a bronze, silver or gold Walter Fritz medal. Kai was given a silver medal and called one of the best young talents playing in Germany that year.

However, it wasn't only the German Football Association that Kai had impressed. Kai had also managed to catch the attention of the Bayer 04 Leverkusen first-team manager.

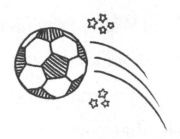

EXAMS VS CHAMPIONS LEAGUE

Roger Schmidt, Bayer's manager at the time, brought Kai into the first team. He had been impressed by the young star. Kai's performances in training only confirmed Schmidt's

belief that Kai was going to play an important role in the future of the club.

On the 15th of October 2016, Kai became Bayer 04 Leverkusen's youngest ever debuting player. Bayer were playing an away tie against SV Werder Bremen. Kai had been named as a substitute option and he remained on the bench for the majority of the game. With the team trailing 2-1 and only a handful of minutes remaining, the coach turned to Kai.

42,100 fans were packed into the Weserstadion with the majority of them routing for SV Werder Bremen. Kai appeared on the field to a chorus of unfriendly chants and roars, but this did not faze him in the slightest. He ran onto the field with the biggest smile on his face, determined to try and claw the game back for his team.

Despite his best efforts, there was only a limited amount of time left on the clock and Kai was unable to change the score. Bayer returned to Leverkusen without any points. But Kai had made his professional

debut and had started on his path to becoming a first-team regular.

Kai did not have to wait long for his next appearance. He traveled to play in a mid week tie in the DFB-Pokal: Germany's cup competition. Bayer's opponents were Sportfreunde Lotte: a third division side and heavy underdogs. Kai played his part in an enthralling tie that finished level at full time. The match then went to extra time and eventually penalties. Kai did not shy away from the high-pressure situation and put his hand up to take one of the penalties.

The home crowd was roaring, with chants and jeers flying from every corner of the ground to try and put Kai off. But Kai focussed on one thing. He was visualizing exactly where he was going to fire the ball and how good it would feel when it smacked against the net. Tuning out the noise, Kai ran up to the ball and placed it into the bottom left-hand corner with precision. His coolness displayed a confidence and ability way beyond his teenage years.

Despite scoring, Bayer were defeated in the penalty shoot-out in a massive upset by Sportfreunde Lotte. The defeat hurt Kai, but he did not have long to dwell on its bitter taste. Instead, on the long journey home to Leverkusen, Kai had to use the time to study. The very next morning he had exams at school!

Kai arrived at his school the next morning and joined the line outside of the main hall. He tried  his best to hide how tired he was, but an unstoppable yawn burst out of him. One of his friends in the line tapped his shoulder.

"Unlucky about last night," said his friend. "Great penalty."

"Thanks," said Kai, holding back a yawn.

Hearing them talking, an examiner walked over to the pair and shushed them.

"There's an exam still going on in there," he told them. "We need total silence." The examiner's annoyance quickly disappeared, replaced by a look of recognition. His frown gave way to a smile upon realizing who Kai was. "Aren't you Kai Havertz?"

Kai nodded.

"Could you sign this bit of paper for me, please? I'm a huge Bayer fan!"

Kai signed the paper. When the examiner left, Kai and his friend had to cover their mouths with their hands to stop themselves from laughing.

While Kai's exam day didn't go incredibly smoothly, his soccer career certainly did. During the 2016/2017 season, Kai made twenty-four appearances for the club, scoring four goals and providing six assists. And he didn't stop there. In the 2017/2018, season Kai made thirty appearances, scoring three goals and providing nine assists.

Kai was also given his first Champions League start, in an away game against Atlético Madrid. Although Beyer lost the match, Kai made an impact with his defensive plays. However, he had to miss the second leg as it fell on an exam day, and even a Champions League quarterfinal isn't a good enough excuse to get out of an exam! But the

weeks passed by and Kai made his way through his exams. Finally he was finished with school and could focus all of his attention on soccer.

6
DIE
MANNSCHAFT

From a young age, Kai was seen as having the potential to make the senior national team. Here was a talented soccer player who could follow in the footsteps of legendary German midfielders such as Michael Ballack and Toni Kroos. Kai had

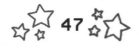

already played for the national youth teams. He played over thirty matches for the Germany U16, U17 and U19 sides, before being called up to play in Germany's senior team. He was such a talent that he completely bypassed the U21 setup and found himself in a team with Germany's most talented soccer players.

Joachim Löw, Germany's team manager, brought Kai into the squad that was taking part in the very first Nations League. Germany's first opponent in the tournament were the reigning World Cup champions: France. Kai remained on the substitutes bench for this 0-0 draw, but he still learned from the experience. He'd been training with Germany's top players and was beginning to understand how the national team worked together. He learned how to mold his style to offensive and defensive tactics, and how to adapt to a completely different style of play from his club. Germany had another game only three days after the match with France.

This time it was a friendly against Peru. Would Kai get a chance to play in this one?

Once again Kai was named on the substitutes bench, but he held onto hope. With this being a friendly, there was every chance that he could get some game time. He was desperate to make his debut appearance for the senior national team.

The first half flew by in a flash, and the teams headed into the changing rooms. Peru had taken the lead in the 22nd minute, but Germany had quickly responded

with Julian Brandt equalizing in the 25th minute. Every time Kai looked up to the scoreboard, it was as if the minutes were passing by in double speed. No matter how hard he tried to concentrate on the game there was one question on his mind: am I going to get a chance to play?

As the second half started, the clock refused to slow down. Nico Schulz scored a second goal for Germany in the 85th minute. His shot somehow squeezed underneath the Peruvian goalkeeper and trickled across the line. With the clock running down, Kai's hope was starting to fade. He'd enjoyed the opportunity to join up with the squad, but couldn't hide his disappointment that he'd not been able to get onto the field. Then, before the clock reached the 90th minute, there was a shout from across the technical area.

"Kai!" shouted Löw, trying to make his voice heard among the  thousands of cheering German fans. "I want you to warm up. You're coming on for the last few minutes."

Kai had never stood up so fast. He sprinted up and down the touchline, stretching and warming up his muscles before making his way back to the bench. At the next stoppage of play, the fourth assistant held up the subs board and Löw placed his hand on Kai's shoulder.

"Congratulations," he said. "Show them what you can do."

Kai ran onto the field and joined in with the action. He was no longer just Kai the youngster playing soccer in his grandad's garden. He was no longer just a domestic soccer player. He was now an international soccer player.

The handful of minutes he was on the field were a success. His determination and passion shone through as he helped Germany hold onto their lead and take the win. Kai, proudly wearing the German colors, soaked in every last second he could. He was one of the last to leave the field at the end of the game. As the fans in the stadium began to leave and the TV crew started to pack away,

Kai made his way down the tunnel. Away from the cameras, he smiled and wiped a tear away from his cheek.

7
TOP SCORING MIDFIELDER

Kai returned to Bayer 04 Leverkusen
and played his best season yet.
The boy wonder had a key role in
the club's 2018/2019 Bundesliga
campaign. He scored seventeen goals
and provided four assists, making
him the third top goalscorer in the

entire league. He came just behind
the clinical strikers Paco Alcácer,
with eighteen goals, and Robert
Lewandowski, with twenty-two goals.

In the previous two seasons,
Bayer had failed to qualify for the
Champions League. However, with
one of the best attacking talents in
the league, they had every chance of
making it this time round. The race
for a spot in the top four went all the
way to the last day of the season ...

Spurred on by Kai, Bayer were in
with a chance of finishing fourth
in the Bundesliga and claiming a

Champions League ticket for next year. Kai had scored six goals in six games and was on one of the hottest scoring streaks of his career. He needed his streak to continue to help his team get over the line.

The three sides fighting Bayer for the fourth spot were Borussia Mönchengladbach, Eintracht Frankfurt and VfL Wolfsburg. But Bayer had the advantage. As long as they bettered or matched their opponents' results, they would claim victory and send themselves on a European tour in the following

season. Standing in the way of Kai and Bayer's hopes were Hertha BSC. This was a mid-table side with nothing to play for on the last day, other than to chalk up a win over a highly rated side in Bayer.

The referee blew his whistle and the match kicked off at the Olympiastadion in Berlin. The majority of the fans inside the stadium were not rooting for Bayer to succeed, but that didn't bother Kai.

 He was on a mission to send his team to the Champions League.

In the 28th minute, Bayer's central defender Jonathan Tah sent a long pass over the Hertha defense. Quicker to react than anyone else, Kai ran onto the pass and volleyed the ball with his left foot. *Goal!* Kai celebrated behind the goal and cupped his ears to the taunts and jeers of the Hertha fans.

But Bayer's lead in the match did not last long. Only a handful of minutes later it was the Hertha fans who were celebrating. Valentino Lazaro latched onto a chance ball and cushioned it into the net, making the score 1-1.

Hertha had struck back fast, but so, too, did Bayer. Lucas Alario restored Bayer's lead with a fine finish, flicking the ball past the onrushing keeper to make the score 1-2 to Bayer.

Not long after this, the teams went into the locker rooms at halftime. As it stood, Bayer had a firm grip on fourth place in the league. With forty-five minutes still to play, though, all of that could easily change. A couple of goals from

Hertha would change the picture entirely. Bayer were so close, but still so far.

Kai and his teammates put any doubts behind them in a blistering second-half performance. Ten minutes after the restart, Brandt scored a screamer from distance. The ball shot through the air and curled into the top corner, stunning both the home and the away supporters. Alario then went on to score both his second *and* third goals of the match for a hat trick.

Bayer won the match 1-5, took the full three points and rightfully claimed their place as the fourth best side in the Bundesliga. In the next season, the club were going to be playing in the Champions League! For that honor, they owed a lot to Kai Havertz.

JACK OF ALL TRADES

While Kai and Bayer's 2018/2019 campaign had been a success, the same could not be said about the 2019/2020 season. Bayer had drawn a challenging Champions League group with the likes of Italian giants Juventus, Spanish side Atlético

Madrid and Russia's Lokomotiv Moscow. Bayer fell to three straight defeats before rallying later on for a chance of making the knockout rounds, with wins against Lokomotiv and Atlético. But despite their efforts, Kai and Bayer were knocked out of the Champions League.

Bayer finished third in their group but were given a second chance in Europe via the Europa League. In this competition, eight third-place teams who were eliminated from the Champions League group stages were dropped into the Europa League. Kai and Bayer found much more success there with Kai scoring four goals and providing two assists en route to the quarterfinals. But it was at this stage that their European tour came to its end. They were defeated 2-1 by the Italian side Inter Milan.

While Bayer didn't get their hands on a European trophy, they had a chance at glory much closer to home. The first match in this season's DFB-Pokal took Kai back into a cup title fight. Bayer 04 Leverkusen had been drawn away to none other than Alemannia Aachen: the first professional side to give Kai an opportunity in soccer.

As the match was so close to Kai's home, his family, friends and almost an entire city of people bought tickets to watch. Many of them were diehard Aachen fans who wanted to see their team triumph in the cup, but they were also proud that someone they knew had made it to such heights as Kai. The matchup gave many of them mixed emotions!

Bayer were clear favorites, and in an exciting encounter they defeated the home side 1-4. Kai made a darting run past a tired defense and swung his left foot at the ball. *Goal!* As the ball rippled against the net, Kai fell to the ground and stayed there for a moment. As he stood up, he looked conflicted.

Kai had just achieved a childhood dream by scoring a goal at the New Tivoli stadium—Alemannia Aachen's home ground. He had always

 dreamt of scoring in the yellow and black of the home side, but instead he was scoring the final goal of the game for

Bayer. He was delighted to score, but there was a pinch of sadness in scoring against his childhood team.

Bayer continued to put in strong performances in the following rounds of the DFB-Pokal. They defeated SC Paderborn 07, Vfb Stuttgart, Union Berlin and Saarbrücken to make it all the way to the final. It was the first time that Kai had made it to a cup final. However, it was not going to be an easy match, as their opponents were the mighty Bayern Munich: one of the most successful teams in the Bundesliga.

If Kai and his team were going
to get anything from this match,
they needed to defeat the reigning
champions.

The players shook hands and
prepared for the match in front of an
empty stadium. Due to COVID-19, no
fans were there and every kick and
shout on the field could be heard.

Bayern Munich scored the first
goal of the match with a pinpoint
precision free kick. David Alaba,
the Swiss center-back with an
unrivalled left foot, curled the ball
past the diving Lukáš Hrádecký

and into the Bayer net. Less than ten minutes later, Bayern Munich doubled their lead. Serge Gnabry made an unstoppable run past the Bayer defense and effortlessly scored his team's second goal. Kai and his teammates were 2-0 down in the first twenty-five minutes, but Kai wasn't going to let this early setback stop him.

"We're better than this," said Kai, during halftime.

The rest of the players, even those much older than him, looked to their star player for guidance.

"We can turn this game around. We mustn't give up!" said Kai, trying to energize and organize his team.

Kai was able to steady the sinking ship, but only temporarily. In the 59th minute, Lewandowski scored Bayern Munich's third goal from an impressive volley outside of the box. His shot was so powerful that although it was aimed directly at the goalkeeper, it wriggled out of his grasp and over the line.

Bayer were able to recover some hope thanks to a Sven Bender header that hit the back of the net. But that

hope was quickly squashed by a strong defense and a fourth Bayern Munich goal. In the 89th minute, Lewandowski grabbed his second goal of the game with a delicate chip over the keeper.

It seemed like defeat was coming, but Kai refused to give up. His energy and enthusiasm rubbed off on the team, and in the final minute of the match, Bayer were awarded a penalty. Kai was nominated to take it by his teammates and he coolly struck the ball into the top corner past Manuel Neur. However, after scoring he did not celebrate. Instead, he kicked at the air in frustration. He had scored, and he had played well, but at the end of the match he was taking home a runners-up medal and not lifting his first ever professional trophy.

As he had been in previous seasons, Kai was a shining light for the club during their Bundesliga campaign. Kai could not match his impressive tally from the season before, but he still managed to score fourteen goals and provide six assists.

While in the previous year Kai had been able to lead his team to a fourth-place finish, the same was not achieved during the 2019/2020 season. Bayer finished fifth— only two points outside of the top four. They would be playing in the Europa League next year and not the Champions League.

As a result of his consistent performances at such a young age, Kai had received the nickname *Alleskönner*—a German word referring to someone who is good at many things. He was viewed as a midfield maestro and one of the best that the country had seen for years. He had the strategic and bullish nature of Michael Ballack combined with a deadly eye for the goal.

With these consistent performances, word had quickly spread across the soccer community. Kai was no longer Bayer's secret, but a player known around the world as one of the most promising young talents. When the door closed on a disappointing season with Bayer, the biggest clubs came

knocking offering new possibilities.
Only a handful of clubs were able to
afford Kai's high price tag. Would
anyone go deep enough into their
pockets to tempt Bayer to part ways
with their young talent?

9
LONDON BOUND

Due to the COVID-19 pandemic, the transfer budgets of most clubs had been drastically cut. With additional costs and money lost without ticket sales, it appeared that few clubs would be able to make any huge transfers. Kai enjoyed playing for

Bayer 04 Leverkusen, and another year at the club was never out of the question. But it was obvious to all that Kai's talent was worthy of a team that could fight for the highest honors. He was a soccer superstar who wouldn't look out of place playing for the best teams in world soccer. Many expected Kai to move to one of the German giants such as Bayern Munich, or to a Spanish great like Real Madrid or Barcelona. But, instead, his move was to a team that came entirely ... out of the blue.

Chelsea FC, one of the biggest clubs in the Premier League, put in an offer for Kai. They were an established team with a decorated and successful history, but they were not so successful at the time. The club was in a transition period. In the previous year they had hired Frank Lampard, their former star midfielder, as their manager. Lampard was a player that Kai admired and had watched countless times on the TV as a child.

While many clubs were holding back their cash, the same could

not be said about Chelsea. Due to
a transfer ban, Chelsea had been
unable to bring in players the
previous summer. All of that spare
cash was burning a hole in their
billionaire owner's pocket, and he
spent it with glee during the summer
of 2020. The club had already signed
Timo Werner, Hakim Ziyech, Ben
Chilwell and Thiago Silva. In a
matter of months, they seemed to be
transforming from a club of the past
to a club of the present.

Kai was out on a walk in the
summer sun when his phone started

 to vibrate in his pocket. He looked at his phone, not recognizing the foreign number. He answered it anyway.

"Hello?"

"Hello, Kai."

Kai recognized the voice in an instant. It was Frank Lampard. In an attempt to convince Kai to join Chelsea, the manager had decided to make a phone call.

"I'd love for you to come and play for us," said Lampard. "I'd have come to see you in person but there's a little something called COVID stopping me from taking a plane right now!"

Kai laughed. "Yeah, that has been a little bit of an issue, hasn't it?"

"We're trying to build something special: a team filled with young, talented and determined players," Lampard continued. "We want to be successful in the Premier league, not just in the next two years but for the next ten. With you on our team, I think that would be a real possibility."

"That sounds exciting. I'd love to help take the Blues back to the top," said Kai. "I'll talk to my family, but this

would be an incredible opportunity.
I'll get back to you soon."

Kai continued on his walk and
thought things over. Of all places,
was his future going to be in
London, under the management of
an iconic midfielder and in a new
and developing team? The longer
Kai thought about it, and the more
talks he had with those close to
him, it all started to make sense.
All of the puzzle pieces were slowly
fitting into place. This had
the potential to be a
big move—a career-

defining step in Kai's hunt for soccer glory.

Kai made his mind up and wanted the move, and the clubs finalized the transfer. In the end, Chelsea parted with a club record fee of over £72 million to bring Kai to Stamford Bridge. It took their transfer spend to over a whopping £200 million in one summer. It was a clear statement that Chelsea wanted to be back at the very top of world soccer.

Kai said goodbye to his teammates at Bayer Leverkusen and set off on a life-changing move—not just to a new club, but to an entirely new country. It was exciting to know that he would not be going through all of this on his own. After Chelsea's spending spree, he was going to be one of many new faces arriving at the club.

But before Kai moved to London, he had to say goodbye to the people who meant the most to him. Kai was dropped off at the airport with his whole family there to see him off—his father, his mother, his siblings and even the family dog!

"Well, this is it!"
said Kai. Before he
could say another word,
his mother wrapped her arms
around him and squeezed him
as tightly as she could.

"Stay safe," she said, wiping a tear
from her cheek.

"I promise," said Kai. He said
goodbye to each of his family and
made sure to reach into the back of
the car to give the dog a goodbye
scratch. "I'm not going to the moon,
you know. You can all visit my new
place in London!"

With one last wave, Kai's family drove off. Kai smiled, wheeled his suitcase to the check-in desk and headed off on his next adventure.

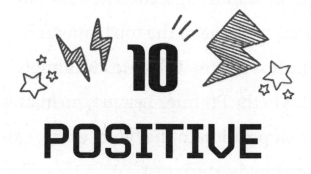

10
POSITIVE

Although millions had been spent on
Chelsea's team, not much changed
in terms of performance as the
2020/2021 season began. Despite the
arrival of obvious talent, the players
struggled to gel together. Kai found
the demands and physicality of the
Premier League difficult to cope with.

In the Bundesliga, the difference in quality between the top teams and the less successful teams was huge. But in the Premier League, no matter their position in the table, every team provided a stern test.

While Kai struggled to make a positive impact on the team during Premier League matches, he did not have as many difficulties in the English Soccer League Cup. Chelsea were matched against Championship side Barnsley in the third round of the competition, and Kai was handed a rare game start. He repaid

his manager's trust by putting on a breathtaking performance for a 6-0 home win. Kai scored an impressive hat trick, justifying his high price tag and showing the Chelsea fans and spectators just how talented he was. But after this show of good form, Kai continued to struggle.

Players often find it difficult to settle into new surroundings and cultures, and it can take time for a player to find their form. But this knowledge did not give Kai any comfort. He wanted to win at all costs and spent hours upon hours on the training ground trying to improve. However, in November he was stopped in his tracks by something entirely out of his control.

Kai tested positive for COVID-19.

While some people do not suffer extreme sickness due to the virus, the same could not be said for Kai. The virus kept Kai in bed for two and a half weeks with a flu worse than he had ever experienced before. He was also hundreds of miles away from his family and only able to speak to them over video or phone calls. Despite this tough period, Kai was able to

fight off the virus, and he started to recover. Unfortunately, because the virus had hit him so hard, the recovery took far longer than he would have liked.

"Welcome back, Kai," said Werner, a fellow German signing, when Kai returned to the training field. "You holding up okay?"

Kai nodded and smiled back at his friend. Kai was wearing a pair of gloves and a hat to fight off the winter cold. Werner brought his hands to his face and blew on them. His breath clouded due to the low temperature, escaping through the cracks of his fingers and vanishing into the morning haze. Kai greeted the rest of his teammates and lined up in front of the coaches.

"Nice to have you back Kai," said one of the coaches. "Now let's all warm up. Give me three laps around the field to get your blood pumping."

The players took off around the sidelines. Kai was never the fastest player in the team, but he was also never the slowest. Now Kai could feel his lungs working overtime. His heart was beating fast and the muscles in his legs ached. The first few training sessions were hard, but slowly Kai started to regain his fitness. He worked closely with the medical and fitness teams at the club. It took a further three weeks for Kai to feel like he was at 100% again.

During this time, the club was not doing well. Despite the fans' love for Lampard, and the talented crop of players at the club, the hard truth was that things were not going to plan. As such, the board made the

decision that Lampard's time as manager was over. Kai was disappointed to lose a coach he admired and who had brought him to the club, but he knew that turnarounds were a common feature of professional soccer.

As a replacement for Lampard, the club hired a famous German manager: Thomas Tuchel. The new coach brought fresh ideas and tactics to the team, which had an immediate impact on the club. Chelsea began to pick up speed and became a solid defensive team. This laid the groundwork for the club's attackers to thrive.

Under Tuchel's management, and past the bad fortune of his illness, Kai started to feel like himself again. He was getting more minutes in games and everyone was playing with confidence. The momentum was so great that the club managed to shock everyone and make it all the way to the Champions League final. In a season of multiple low points,

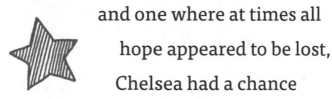 and one where at times all hope appeared to be lost, Chelsea had a chance

at winning the most sought-after trophy in European soccer. With his form improved, could Kai Havertz lead Chelsea to a Champions League triumph?

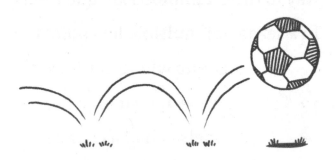

11
PERFECTION
IN PORTO

In Porto, Portugal on 29th May 2021, Chelsea met Manchester City for an all-English Champions League Final. Both sides came onto the field to a roar from the fans. The match was played at the Estádio do Dragão with a smaller crowd than usual due to

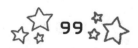

COVID-19, but that did not stop the fans who could attend from cheering as loudly as possible.

In a difficult first season in England, Kai now had an incredible opportunity. He'd gotten used to life in a new country, witnessed the sacking of the manager that bought him over and had to fight off a deadly virus. And despite all of that, Kai was ninety minutes away from lifting the most important trophy in European soccer.

Standing in his way were the Premier League champions.

Manchester City were the clear favorites. They had walked their way to the league title, but Chelsea could not be written off. While they had struggled to perform at the start of the season, they had come into form at exactly the right time for the European competition. In a single knockout match, anything could happen.

The referee blew the whistle and the game kicked off. Manchester City had the first big chance. Their goalkeeper, Ederson, found Raheem Sterling with a pinpoint long-distance kick. The nimble forward caught the Chelsea defense off guard. Sterling chased after the ball and brought it into the penalty box. But before he could shoot, Chelsea's Reece James nudged him off, giving their goalkeeper, Édouard Mendy, time to narrow the shooting range and defend the ball. While the team in sky blue had not scored from the chance, it showed just how quickly they could cause damage.

Chelsea fired back with a chance of their own. Mason Mount stole the ball and ran to the edge of the penalty box.

Kai and Timo were sprinting as fast as they could to set themselves up for a shooting opportunity. Mount decided to play the ball in for Timo, who struck the ball at goal, but it went directly into Ederson's hands. That was a big chance missed for Chelsea.

The teams went back and forth in a thrilling and tense first half—attack after attack, wave after wave, but who could break the deadlock? Ben Chilwell played a neat pass to Mount on the halfway line. On the counterattack, Kai burst through the center circle and into the opposition

half. Mount played an accurate through ball to Kai. He carried the ball toward the goal and within seconds a blur of bright pink came running at him. Ederson, in his pink goalkeeper gear, tried to take the ball from Kai. But Kai knocked it past him! Ahead there was now an open goal and only one thing to do. Kai placed the ball with his left foot into the net. *Goal!*

The Chelsea fans erupted with joy and Kai sprinted to the corner to celebrate. In twelve Champions

League appearances, he'd never scored. What a time to break that streak. What a time to score his first goal in a tournament: in the final.

Chelsea held on to the lead and went into halftime only forty-five minutes away from glory. Manchester City threw everything they had at the game in the second half. Chelsea denied them chances with their strong defense. Despite Manchester City's desperation, Chelsea were able to cling on.

As the final whistle blew, Kai was overwhelmed by emotion and fell to his knees. He'd won his first ever professional trophy and had scored the winning goal in a Champions League Final. The coaches and substitutes ran onto the field. They crowded Kai and celebrated with him. Kai Havertz had won the Champions League for Chelsea.

After a night of celebrations, Kai woke up late the next morning. At the hotel in Porto, the players were enjoying breakfast outside with a beautiful view of the city below and plates filled with delicious food. Kai sat down and looked at the scenic

view, but there was something far
more beautiful opposite him on the
table: the Champions League trophy.

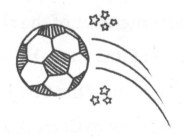

12

EURO 2020

After finishing the 2020/2021 season in the best form of his life, Kai hoped to continue playing at his best while representing Germany. Kai had been selected as a member of the squad to participate in Euro 2020. He wasn't the only member of the Chelsea team who was heading to Germany's camp.

His teammates Werner and Antonio Rüdiger were in the squad too.

In a team filled with young and emerging talent, confidence was building around this German squad. Historically, Germany had often performed well in major international tournaments. However, they had not had much success in recent years, with the team embarrassingly finishing bottom of their group during the 2018 World Cup. But history wasn't something that Kai needed to worry about. All he needed to do was perform in the present and restore glory to a great soccer nation.

Germany was drawn in the so called "Group of Death". In major tournaments, teams have to battle it out in a group stage made up of four teams. Each team tries to make it to the knockout rounds. For this tournament, Germany had found themselves in what was considered the toughest group of them all. To progress from the group, they needed to perform well against Portugal, France and Hungary.

The first side they met was France:

the reigning World Cup champions and favorites for the tournament. France were a team with years of historic success on their side. They had talented players in their ranks such as fellow rising star Kylian Mbappé. In fact, in the tunnel before the game kicked off, Mbappé took Kai by surprise. Kai was kneeling to tighten his cleats when the forward tapped him on the shoulder.

"I watched the Champions League Final," said Mbappé. "Great goal."

"Thanks," said Kai. "I'm hoping to score another one today."

Kylian grinned. "We'll see about that. Have a good game."

In the 19th minute of the match, France's Paul Pogba played a delicate through ball with the outside of his right foot into the left of the penalty box. Lucas Hernandez brought the ball under his control and fired it across the box. Kai watched helplessly from midfield, unable to stop what was about to happen. Germany's defender Mats Hummels stuck out his leg in an attempt to stop the attack, but with Mbappé lurking behind him, all he could do was put the ball into his own net.

It was a tightly fought contest. Germany were unable to turn the tie around and started the tournament with a defeat. But their competition was far from over. If they could play well in their remaining two matches, then they had every chance of progressing to the knockout rounds. They needed their young star to shine.

Germany faced Portugal next, in need of a great result. Cristiano Ronaldo and his teammates, fresh off a victory against Hungary, would not be easy opponents. The match did not get off to the best start for the Germans, with Ronaldo scoring a tap-in on the 15th minute. Kai and his team needed to play to the best of their ability, and they certainly did. Spurred on by Kai, the team rallied and fought back.

In the 35th minute, Robin Gosens fired a cross into the box and Kai was ready to pounce. In an attempt to stop Kai from scoring, Rúben Dias tried to intercept but could only send the ball into his own net. *Goal!* The match was level at 1-1.

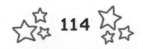

Only a few minutes later, Kai was in the opposition penalty box causing havoc. He cleverly flicked the ball across the Portuguese penalty box and found the onrushing Joshua Kimmich. Kimmich fired the ball at the goal, and once more it was met by a Portuguese foot rather than a German one! The ball found its way into the back of the net. After two Portuguese own goals, Germany were now in the lead.

In the second half, Kai put his name on the scoresheet. Another thunderous Gosens cross flashed across goal and Kai passed it into the net, making the score 1-3 to Germany. Kai had scored his first goal at a major international tournament. Gosens grabbed a goal for himself, and Portugal replied with a late effort from Diogo Jota, but as the final whistle blew, the match was Germany's. It finished 2-4 and Germany's tournament hopes were back alive. On a stage with one of soccer's greatest ever players,

Ronaldo, it was Kai who had come out with the victory. At the end of the match,

Ronaldo kicked at the turf in frustration. Kai approached him with his hand held out.

"You were a nightmare to play against," said Ronaldo, appreciating Kai's gesture and shaking his hand.

"I enjoyed the game," said Kai with a smile.

"Well I didn't," joked Ronaldo. "Congratulations. Looks like it's going down to the final group match."

"Hopefully we both get through," said Kai.

"I like the sound of that," said Ronaldo. "But if we meet in the competition again, don't expect to have that grin on your face."

Germany's third and final group stage tie was against Hungary—a side that they were expected to beat. But Hungary had other ideas. The visiting side took the lead thanks to a header from Ádám Szalai in the 11th minute. It was a lead that they held on to all the way up until the 66th minute.

Hummels rose higher than the players around him to meet a cross in the Hungarian box and headed the ball at the goal. On the line, being pushed by a Hungarian defender, all

Kai had to do was guide the ball into the net with his head. *Goal!* It wasn't the most difficult goal Kai had scored, but it was an important one. The score was 1-1, but the match did not stay level for long.

Straight after the kickoff to reset the match, Hungary shocked everyone by taking the lead again. András Schäfer reacted quickest to a through ball and headed the ball past Neur in goal. With France and Portugal tied and taking away equal points from their match

elsewhere, Germany were going to be eliminated from the tournament.

However, in the 84th minute Germany got a lifeline. Leon Goretzka saved Germany by equalizing and helping his team finish the match level. This made sure that Germany went through to the knockout rounds, setting up a mouth-watering knockout tie with England.

In front of a lively 43,000 fans at their home stadium at Wembley, England proved too strong. Goals from Raheem Sterling and Harry Kane eliminated Germany from the competition. Kai played well during the match, and at one point came close to scoring—only being denied a goal by a flying save from Jordan Pickford.

It was the end of an era for Germany as the game was the last under their manager, Löw. Under Löw's leadership, the Germany team had excelled and achieved great things. But as time drove forward, those successes were firmly in the rearview mirror. With a new-look German side, Kai as the leading light and new manager Hansi Flick, the future looked bright. Although success had not come their way in this competition, with a rising star in their team, many hoped that future trophies were not far away.

13
ROAD TO QATAR 2022

After a year unlike any other, Kai returned home to see his family. With COVID restrictions finally lifting, he couldn't wait to see his family in person rather than on a video call. But before reuniting with them, Kai needed to visit somewhere important to him.

On a field near the house where Kai grew up, there were four of Kai's favorite animals: donkeys. In this group there was a donkey that he had saved from slaughter when it was just 8 months old. Staring out into the damp field, Kai thought twice about wearing his expensive white sneakers and instead pulled his wellington boots from the back of his car. Leaving the car, he hopped over a fence, boots splashing in the mud, before picking up some straw. One of the donkeys wandered over to Kai. He fed it with one hand and stroked its head with the other.

"Do you remember me?" said Kai. "Sorry I've been away for so long. You won't believe the year I've had."

Kai continued to feed the donkeys and before he knew it, the sun was starting to set. He'd been there for over an hour! Kai said his goodbyes and left the field. It was now time to drive over to see his family.

As he drove through familiar streets, Kai was filled with nostalgia. He remembered childhood matches at parks, early-morning and late-night training sessions with close friends. That young boy had made it all the way from those muddy fieldes to a Champions League final. As he drove, his suitcase was not filled with dirty clothes and soccer cleats, but designer wear and a Champions League winners' medal.

Kai arrived outside of his parents' new house and parked his car. He made his way to the door and went to press the doorbell. Before he could do so, the door flung open and his mother leapt at him.

"Kai!" she said, wrapping her arms around him. After the hug, she stepped back and examined him. "Why are you in wellington boots? There's mud on your jeans!"

Kai looked down to see that he had completely forgotten to change back into his sneakers. Some mud from the field had splashed up past his knees.

"Did you go and see the *donkeys* before your own mother?" she said, crossing her arms.

Like a mischievous child, Kai smiled back at her. "You caught me."

The young boy from Aachen had achieved so much at such a young age. He'd starred in his home country at Bayer Leverkusen, became Chelsea's record transfer and played for Germany in a major international tournament.

With years of his career still to play, there are many more assists, goals and records for Kai to break.